COLOR ME FREE

VIRGINIA PULLIAM

BALBOA.
PRESS

A DIVISION OF HAY HOUSE

ISBN: 978-1-4525-5698-7 (sc)
ISBN: 978-1-4525-5699-4 (e)

Library of Congress Control Number: 2012914758

Balboa Press books may be ordered through booksellers or by contacting:

Balboa Press
A Division of Hay House
1663 Liberty Drive
Bloomington, IN 47403
www.balboapress.com
1-(877) 407-4847

Printed in the United States of America

Balboa Press rev. date: 08/14/2012

Table of Contents

ONE

Country Lover

My man works hard all week
Dirty boots and stinky feet
My Friday Night special love so sweet
Nothing is more complete
Passionate kisses the suck lip kind
The kind that makes your juices flow
I close my eyes and float in the pleasure of his skillful hands
He gives me what I want nothing left undone
He loves me into a peaceful sleep
Early morning Saturday sunrise
Skillful hands more powerful than the night before
Moving magically giving pleasure awakening
All passion in my body
Skillful Country Lover of mind
Up by nine breakfast cooked
My man turns and gives me a look
With a smile as bright as the sunlit sky
In bed by dust all chores are done
He passionately holds me until we are done
Sunday dinner received with Grace
Sunday night passion, sleep to rest another week of hard work
Dirty boots and stinky feet
1995

Too Love

Intrigued, I am with you
I like the way you listen to me
The way you here my heart
I like the way we sit and talk
So much passion flowing
I like the way time has given us wisdom
To see us through
I like the way you feel in my space
I hope you feel it too
I like knowing hope is real
I like the way love has free will
Intrigued, I am with you
2002

(Man) Song

You say you want to be my (man) song
When you are bound to another lyrically
You want me to come to you and play on your keys
While you play sweet melodies on my strings
You want me to sing melodies to your keys
A flat, **B** flat and sometimes **E**
When I look at you, I must say, my notes sang
But what would this mean to play melodies on your keys
Will you reel me in with sweetness and warmth?
To leave my fingers tired to feel every joint
When I play melodies, I want the listeners to hear every word
I play my cords from my heart
When I touch my strings I want to feel every part
So, I open my stage to your keys ivory's black and white, on my strings
Now the melodies of my strings are playing sweet songs to your keys
Together our songs will be bound forever, with sweetness and melody
Are you pleased?
April 2003

Happy Birthday Song to my Son

It's your birthday yes it's your birthday
And I love you
Oh how I love you, my baby
Twenty-five years, I have known your love
You make me proud to be a Mom
To be a Mom, to be a Mom
I couldn't have asked for a better son
You are the love of my life
As I sit here and remember the day you were born
Big brown eyes, chocolate brown skin, like liquid
All these years I have watched you grow into the Man you are today
Today on your birthday
I want you to know, I am sooooooo proud of your growth!
I smile the day you were born
I smiled, cried and frown as I watched you grow
There was always a bright light in my heart and on my mind
Whenever I think of you or when someone mentions your name
I am the happiest and proudest mother in all the land
To be able to call you my Son the Man
Love and kisses to you everyday of my life
Happy Birthday, Love Mom
May 16, 2004

His Love for Her

When he looks into her eyes, he understands why he loves
her with his soul
You see, God told him so
God says, "Love with your heart and put heart into your love"
The love you share will be like a seed that sprouts after a rain,
On a cool summer night when all you want to feel is a breeze
Don't be afraid to show her your true heart
For she wants for the gentle breezes to fill her mind
As it enter twines through her heart and makes her weak in her knees
For his love is true it's a gift from God
It's gentle, sweet and moist
It's kind, warm and calming to her soul
It's all she needs to make her feel whole
And in return she gives back tenfold
So he continues to look into her eyes and understands why he loves
her with his SOUL
July 30.2003

Speechless

Last night my man left me speechless
I came home to a bubble bath
With scent that sooths the soul
He washed me smooth and with every stroke his smile was just for me
He held my hand and helps me out
He dried me off as he pampered me
He smoothed me over with silky scented oils
Then he proceeded to dress me
He took me out to eat
We wine and dine as he looked into **my** eyes
When ever our eyes met, we smiled in quiet anticipation of what
was to come
He drove me to the shore, we walked in the sand
As the moonlight, bounced off the ocean waves and the black sky
sparkled with shimmering light
He held my hand while we walked to our suite
He poured me a glass of sparkling wine
He wet his lips and kissed me gentle on my cheek
He smile and took my hand while 'Kem" played on the radio
He held me close and we danced real slow I felt ever movement,
every heart beat
The warmth of his breath on my neck, cheek and ear
With a milky way flowing through my head
He undressed every thread
We lay close and moved with emotion deep, never a word said
My man left me speechless, he left me weak……….
August 1, 2003

Thinking of You

Talking to you is a vision into my life
Sharing hopes and dreams of intimate things
Giving so freely, wanting you close
Feeling your passion around me
I see you're hurt, it is mind
We dream the same dream
We want the same things
Will you let me touch your heart?
Let me give you, what I want and need
Let us set our souls free to fly, to soar to a place of solace and peace
That's only meant for you and me
Open your heart and let me in
So together we can began this journey to a loving place
A place where new beginnings never ends
1995

Timing

I wish there were words to say how blessed I feel you came my way
Life is filled with everlasting changes and sometimes we need to fly in different
direction, to achieve the goals that make us whole
So, when we seek our wholeness and the souls around us, stagnates our goals
The time to leave is evident
Your time in my space has lifted
I know the timing is right for I am able to sing once more
I will soar to my next chapter, as I embrace the shift
I know I can only be defeated my self
If I don't make peace with things, already done
I will keep smiling as I seek what is already mind
November 2005

Love Jones Dream

When we first met, I was invisible to your eyes
But I said to myself that's a Love Jones Dream come true
Our path crossed from time to time, small talk was all we spoke
Then one day we stopped to see and there were feeling stirring in the air
In my mind a Love Jones Dream you continue to be
We spoke again and small talk transcend
In your eyes a spark arouse and invisible I was no more
The more we talked the more I new the Love Jones Dream
is real inside my heart
One day I saw how you looked at me
A look, never before would you let me see
That look was priceless
Oh! How special was it, it was all in my dream
Will this Love Jones Dream come true?
July 17, 2003

Hour Glass

Her beauty is that of an hourglass, with movement slow as the grains of sand
Her thinking is deep as Webster
Her skin smooth as glass
With each movement of sand she will lure you in, and keep you until time pass
And once the sand has stopped, intoxicated by every drop, turn he rover and start from the top
We call her houri, a beautiful and voluptuous woman
Beauty untouched by hourglass sand
September 16, 2003

Houri (hoor'e~) a beautiful and voluptuous woman

A Poem for...................

I have known you only a short time and I have watched your spirit grow
I see this smile developing in your heart and your kindness touch me so
The anger you seem to manage with solitude and prayer
Your faith in Jehovah will surely keep you there
It warms me to see you struggle and strive for peace and
wellness for your heart
I always saw your beauty no matter how cloudy the stare
I always prayed for your peace of mind even if I could not be there
I don't question my place in life because God will bring me through
He will let me know when love is real
It is in my heart and now I am sure it always it will be apart of what
we share
So continue to let your heart open and your spirit grow
Jehovah is your salvation and he will continue to let you know
You are a special person, you have the ability to love and be loved
So never give up on yourself, your passion or you peace
The joy you seek on this earth is truly at your reach
March 18, 2003

If I

If I could lay my head my head upon your chest
If I could rest my body in your arms
If I could close my eyes and dream
I would dream a sweet love song
I would let my heart touch your heart, and dance sweet melodies
thought the night
If I could smile at sunrise it would put me at a sweet, peaceful rest
October 2001

Love

I am in love with a man I can't have
Not because he is married, engaged or gay
I am in love with a man in pain
Pain he holds from the past
It takes courage to fall in love
It takes self empowerment to get over pain
It takes a strong mind and a gentle heart to forgive
It takes faith in God to rebuild
It takes two passionate hearts to love again
So fine the courage, the self empowerment
Learn to forgive and free your mind
Fine strength in your faith and passion in your
Love will come in, fill your heart and never part
April 2002

My Man

My man is my friend
But he don't belong to me
He don't come with misguided tendencies
He just comes to love me
He don't bring gifts, nothing to impress
He just brings love, it is all for me
You se, he don't belong to me
Days gone by we may not meet
Time is getting close, it time for us to see,
a love like ours is just a friendship deep
You see he don't belong to me
Love is good, friendship at bit best
Deep conversation is sometimes all we seek
Motivation from me to him makes us lifetime friends
You see he don't belong to me
He is very much a part of me
My man is truly my friend
But you see he don't belong to me
1999

Virginia Pulliam

Who Will It Be?

Who will it be?
The one to touch my heart
The one to hold my hand
Who will it be the one?
The one to make me sing
The one to touch my intellect
Who will be the one?
The one to love a rainbow, a sunrise and sunset
Who will be the one?
The one to open his heart to my life
The to see me whole, happy, sad and fragile and know these are my strength
Who will be the one?
The one who knows God with fear and love
The one who will respect me with moral and ethical insight
Who will it be?
November 24, 2005

Memories

I once loved a memory
I loved it well
Six years passed memory, still there
We can hold onto dreams but life doesn't stop
Memories are the pass
Put them in a box
Keep moving on because life is great
Open your heart to new things
New memories we'll make
Six years is a long time to love a memory well
What's in this memory to keep you there?
Give it up, let it go
Open your heart to new memories
Be free make peace
It's so hard to love a ghost
1997

Two

The Voices Inside Speaks to Me

The voices comes from within
They are telling the story from which I come
A little girl with big brown eyes and skin the color of caramel
Raised on a farm in Chase City, Virginia
Humble beginning with a passion to be heard
Being the middle child, almost never heard
Not the first born spoil to death
Or the last born who got all the love
Just the middle child trying to fine my way
Discipline was all around, not feeling the love
That was mind to feel
I raise my voice through my poems
The voices inside came out in word
Therapeutic and calming as I penned my thoughts to be heard
I am struggling to come out
Never to be lost, silent, or in the shadows of others
I will put myself first behind God and strive to finish,
seeking out God's plan
The middle child is who I am
Free to be me

February 25, 2007

First Kiss

Today we kissed for the first time
It sent chilled up and down my spine
Your touch was like fire
I felt my juices flow
I asked myself what do, I do now
So many question, so many doubts
Can I trust him, give my love to him
I think I want to, it almost feels right
I think I will wait, take my time
I want to get to know more about you
Was your heart made for mind?
So, please be patient and let me take my time
For a love that is true, will be good to you
True love will stand the test of time
2000

Complicated

Complicated passion filled with pain
As I let you skate beneath the surface of my brain
Old town funk is the feeling, the kind that keeps you up
When you sleep wet dreams creep into your nightly peace
Complicated passion and we never touched
Did you feel that breeze on your neck or just a mild chill?
Yeah, that's me, slipping into your day dreams
You, thinking about caramel skin dipped in chocolate
Complicated passion, I got you on my mind,
I anticipate your touch,
blue skies, orange lines, the sun rise and set
Candlelight with song sweet as homemade jam
That's the fire that burns and sizzles on my skin
Complicated passion, never enough
Are you a lusted fill Love Jones?
Here to rock my world
Turned into long walks in the rain to hide the tears filled with pain
I crave for your passion and intimate touch
Then, I wonder, how this can be, when you are just an electronic dream
January 25, 2003

Along the Shore

Along the shore is quiet and peaceful
The sound of the waves roars
The seagulls speaks in sequential volume
The sand is cold beneath my feet
The breeze is cool on my face
The sky is filled with a rainbow of clouds
This is the peace I seek and feel within
While we walk in silent hand in hand
I feel the rhythm of the beat
Along the ocean shore
February 12, 2003

First Touch

We swore never to touch
Coffee shops, book stores we would meet
Long talks, sexy smiles, inner beauty we reached
A weekend away we planned words not spoken
There's no master plan, will we cross uncharted sands
There is a whisper inside of loveliness
A silent jazz song, playing in my head
Keeps me humming from my vocal cords
As the Sax sound covers me tenderly
He covered my round with genteel hands
Never once did I question his approach
Eyes closed softly, while we take this magic carpet ride
Riveting my wild side
The magic dust slowed down
The quicken, of my round caved out!
So much for coffee shops, book stores, long talks and sexy smiles
Intimate beauty, lusted filled hands
We crossed over, playing in the sand
March 8, 2003

Yes, I am Silent

Yes, I am silent, for today I listen
I listen to the sounds of the land
I am silent as I listen to the birds sing
I am silent as I listen to the ocean roar
Yes, I am silent, for today I silent
I stopped to listen to a child speak.
For innocent wisdom is sometimes deep
I sit and listen to the children play
As I am amazed at what they say
Yes! I am silent for today I listen
I listen to my surroundings
I listen to my growth
I tune in on unspoken hate and keep my enemies close
Yes. I am silent,
Today I hear God whisper and I am truly trying to listen
Feed on every word
So, today I am silent
I listen quietly to hear God speak
I keep silent, so I may hear his every word
2003

All Things are Blessings

We wonder from day to day just what our lives will bring
Never just excepting our God given strength
If only we could see pass the moment and know,
that tomorrow brings hope, love and wonderful new beginnings
a wealth of powerful blessings
Never ask God why this thing has happen to me
Just trust the power of God
Know you are strong and faith will keep you going
God loves you and holds your hand
2001

Mirror Image

Life is short and uncertain, oh how we waste so much time
Why can't we look in the mirror and except what we see?
Why do we waste so much time, lying and trying to fool others?
Are we so ashamed of whom we are?
Take a deep breath and compose yourself stand tall
Head up, shoulder back
Slowly open your eyes, don't you like what you see
The beautiful person inside, open all closed doors
Listen to the people around you
Take all positive energy in
Start moving all negative energy out
Put distance between the people that don't move you
For they will never be true friends
They will only stand in the way of you being all you can be
Take back what's your, pay attention to God's blessings for you
The power to create your true destiny is within your mirrored self
November 25, 2005

My Pain

No one knows my pain but God and me
No friends to confide in
No one I can trust
What does that say about me?
Is this thing, that cause, me pain so bad?
Would it burn the human flesh?
Would it change the way you think of me?
If you knew would it change your every touch?
Would you finally back away, wanting to forget me?
Would you make up excuses about this or that?
Remember before you walk away.
This very well maybe you one day.
All you would want is a human touch.
1996

My Passion

Early morning skies, the sun over the ocean
Moon and starlit skies
To be able to look into your eyes
To see peaceful quiet times
To hold your hand while we walk, taking in the scenery
To feel the sun as it warms our skin
Good friends we are
You have been there for a decade
We live our life feeling all the passion and joy
This was created for us as we began our life
To be free, to feel our joy and let the blessings come
Let the twinkling stars fill your heart
Let your passion guide your life
Tap into your creativity and your smiles will come from inside
Be Free

You Say I Am an American

You say I am an American
But you brought me here to be a slave
You came into my place dismiss my mate, and pleasure yourself until
you were done
The you separated my family and sold my only son
In a blink of and eye you left me hanging from a tree to die
You say I am an American
When Abraham Lincoln freed the slaves, now I have no where to go
So, I work for free, to repay my debt for the food and the seeds
You say I am an American
You still place traps for me to fail
As you see me grow and flourish through your front door
Old Jim Crow is on your mind, back doors for blacks
White and Black this is the sign
You are just knocking me ten steps back
You say I am an American
Now guilt sets in and sideways you think my black offspring I
must educate
What a slap in the face, for us left behind without a place
When racial tension flares no matter what I do, you still want let
me get there
When powers stand up for a race without a face, slain bodies shows up
Nat Turner, JFK, Malcolm X, H. Rap Brown, Martin Luther King, Jr.
The fight for equality remains…discrimination, segregation,
affirmative action
Qualification is not a must, you still hire lily white before you hire us
You say I am an American
But the fairness of your judicial system I still do trust
A country of the free, when we still have questions about
President-elect (Brush) campaign strategy

A country that's divided by racial stress, hate crimes and still you let them
wear those white hats, burn cross an be free
You say I am an American
When I wake up as a women black or white, double standard is your creed for me.
I am still not free to grace my face at your country club, unless I am an employee
You say I am an American
When 9-11, suck in on me ...lives were lost, what a rude awakening for the land of the free.
Now, you want me to support your cause for War, then, I ask what cause would, that be
To retaliate for 9-11, to control another country resources or just because power says you can
You say I am an American
Well, if freedom is a choice, how could this be, when the "Dixie Chic's" spoke and got band from country radio, you see?
This I just don't understand, how a Country, could invite a world in and treat them better than me in my homeland
You say I am an **American**
So off to war we go where ours sons and daughters will die for the land of the free and they don't even know why
March 18, 2003(5:15 p.m.)-March 19, 2003(10:45 a.m.)

The Flow of Change

Knowledge and wisdom is what makes life flow
We are taken out and in of changing signs, down roads of unknown veins.
Wisdom is the pulse that guides our knowledge well.
Dejavu is the feeling when paths cross over
and spirits haunts your mind.
As your journey proceed and your spirit grows, we become better equipped to defeat the pain, that want let us have the peace we know is ours to keep.
Spiritually we have grown peacefully we speak,
while quiet ecstasy we seek.
Children raised, and have left home with eyes a blaze as they seek the knowledge to know the peace from a Mommy who raised him well
As they recount the time good and bad they know spiritual peace, through grace songs they remember and keep it deep within their hearts
This lets them know the flow of change is God lesson plan and divine growth.
While this woman spread her wings she digs deep into her pass experience the ones that kept her weak.
With new beginnings knowledge keeps her highly favored
As she seeks the excitement from within
This is the balance of change
March 18, 2003

Who Am I?

I am beautiful in my blackness
Like the beat of the African drum
Played on a cool summer night
The sound of a heartbeat filled with passion and fire
Not complicated or complex
Just silky black and smooth
Big eyes, big thigh, pretty
Maybe a glass of wine on the side
There is no drama on my cloud
Just gentle loving and peaceful times
A woman that has your back the way you have mine
So love me sweet and keep it deep
Come, ride this cloud with me
I will always be by your side
2002

THREE

My Journey to Love

We met on an unsafe playing field
We ignore the truth
We where lured together by altruist, effortless and idyllic needs
You want to set boundaries around me
Boundaries that makes me less than real
Disrespected and to all and you say relax and enjoy the moment
My being is more than a moment it is precious and worthy to be real
I set my goals high and you tell me my sex appeal is hypnotic
My beauty intoxicating
How can you love me with boundaries?
When all I want is to be free
January 28, 2003

Eyes Filled With Pain

I feel your pain it used to be mind
I see the way you avoid looking deep into my eyes
If you look into my eyes what do you think you will see
Would you see the same pain that's inside of you?
I see your pain it's in your walk your talk
I watch you do busy work to avoid spending quiet time
I catch you watching me when my back is turned
I wonder what you see when you look at me
Just what could this be that keeps your heart so locked,
un-free to love me?
Sometimes when I look at you I see a little boy in pain
A little boy left by a man that's didn't know how to love
A little boy who craves his mother's attention,
that's now given to a new love
A little boy in fear, communicating his love is hard to much pain
to endure
He just don't know how to understand, no one to explain away his pain
So as a man he asked himself how can someone love me and be true?
How long will it take before they leave me too?
April 10, 2002

Best Friends for Life

Best friends for our hearts connected at childhood with love
A friendship that would last a life time
Not something we ever really thought of
From childhood games to first boy crushes, heartaches and pain
We endear our childhood and continue to grow
We leaned on one another on one another through
dysfunctional beginnings
We didn't even know, we thought it was all normal,
we new we were having fun
Playing in the streets until the street lights came on then off to home
we would run
Time passed miles separated us, different direction we took
Two Gemini's connected with insightfulness, so different
Distance between us but our friendship remains
Best friends for life
June 2003

Where is your Journey?

When you wake up every day where are you going?
What is the first thing you do after you pray?
Yes! I said pray
Do you read the bible before you brush your teeth?
Do you reach over and kiss your spouse while they sleep?
Do you check on your kids before you wash your face?
Do you thank God for waking you up and giving you another day?
Do you smile when you look at the sky?
Are you creative, constructive, destructive or sad?
Do you just sit around on your ass?
Put a smile on your face to start your day and you will be surprised,
what comes back your way
Live from the mountaintop and reach for the stars
Keep God in your heart, no matter how hard
Be creative, inventive; enjoy your journey where ever you are.
With god in your heart and a smile on your face your journey is set
just enjoy the pace
Where is your Journey?
April 2003

On a Trip No Picture for Keepsakes

My father was an alcoholic.
I knew I didn't want to go there.
Caught by a substance, on a trip to free your mind
No pictures to remember the time.
Everyone in the neighborhood was trying all the new drugs
Taking trips, flying high, seeing pink elephant and then they die.
I knew I didn't want to go there
One day I tried some grass, it only made you eat fast
That's not lady like, that not for me
Cocaine, was a man best friend they gave it to you for free
It was an aphrodisiac you see.
But the day I had to buy my own, $50, a bag
Oh! Hell no, I had a shoe fetish my drug of choice.
$50 high bag or $50 for a pair of shoes
The shoe sale won out for me
$50 highs, aint no trip I want to pay for
If I am going to trip on pink elephant while I fly high or maybe
even die
Let my trip have pictures for memories and keepsakes.
April 24, 2005

My Friend

You are such a very special friend
You are truly loved and held close within
You hold my heart and give me love
You guide my passion through a spiritual journey that we both know,
not where we go
We take on the path of unknown passion,
guided by the will of unknown love
As we journey down this course, our hearts grow deeper in love
You look in my eyes and see the beauty inside, the beauty of our love
I know where not this journey will lead
I will hold onto the love and the memories of all the roads we took
to get here
I will always be bless in this moment feeling this love is real
Your friendship has been kind without, judgment or ridicule
Your openness is in my heart
All of your secrets are safe with me
Friends we are bound and safe in spiritual peace we will stay
March 2001

The Journey

I am waiting for my mind to connect with my life
Should I be waiting for my life to connect with my mind?
They keep trying to meet, but most of the time it's such a feat
I can't go anywhere without the two
They just keep struggling and pulling me, I don't know where to
As soon as I think I have found a place for my life and mind to meet
They just take me on another journey of defeat
I want let that stop me from finding my place
It's just another journey to peace and grace
God gave us the power when we were born
We gave ourselves the struggle,
by not believing in the power of faith
It was always there given to us to go on, take your journey and take
your time
One day you will wake up with your mind and your life in the same place
of peace and grace, knowing that the power was yours all the time

FOUR

Eighty

Birthdays are the lines that mapped the journey of the past
Its shows our weakness and our strengths
Like the lines of a tree you stand here before us
Eighty years strong, no other dares to sing your song
We all hum a sweet melody, to be in your present
For the wisdom you share is therapeutic gold
Somehow you managed to take us on a journey of our souls
You are such a comfort zone and a joy to be around
You have let us vent, cry and share our pain; a day in your space
always brings back smiles
You are such a wonderful rainbow you live so we could know life's
journey is with in us
It lives deep in our souls
Ours lives connected for a reason and our friendship has last through
many seasons
I look at you Eighty years strong, so beautiful, elegant and wise
I can truly say to know you is to grow
Happy birthday dear lady

I Pray for You

Salvation is free repentance is an individual's choice
To have the willingness to be a better person, that's me.
Who are you in this world of evilness and schemes?
What makes you think you can hurt me.
God is my saver he gives me Grace
God give me strength to carry on through evil moments created by man
You may cause me sadness you may cause me pain
This is expected from an evil domain
Has life cut you so deep you can't release the pain?
I pray for you with your unexpected learned behavior
I know you are only a man.
You can only release the bowel that erupts from deep inside of you
For you I pray, to know the peace that God can give.
He gives it freely every day!
June 13, 2003

Fear

Want you let me touch your fears
As we dance the night away
As we look into each others eyes, bodies touching,
hearts intertwining
Want you let me touch your fears
I stand before you as the light flickers on the wall,
the glow touches your face so softly
Want you let me touch your fears
The passion rise inside and the wetness comes
We dance in the night, you hold me in your arms, the music stops
Your heart beats loudly in my ear, the candle light flickers on our
naked skin
You lay me down gently on my back, while you sensually look at me
and take it all in
You touch me so lightly with your finger tips as they brush my body
like silk
While you kiss me softly on my nipples, you suck me in an make
me want more
While you reach down between my thighs and feel my river flow
Want you let me touch your fears
As you slide deep inside and feel the warmth of the river flow
Release your fears to the heavens and just let them go
2002

A Letter To Myself

You came into my life at this time perfect time
My life has evolved ad I love the person I have become
I took time to get here, with a little insight from God
I am now free to love from my heart
There are no wrong roads of knowledge, through all we do
One must have the emotional toughness, source of support and the
ability to learn and grow
I often ask God to give me things and he says no
Then I wonder why God I didn't answer my prayers
He was just letting me know, I wasn't ready for the things I was
asking for
I know now All I have gone through has made me strong
Where I am Is where I am suppose to be
My heart is gentle, kind and ready to love the way I want, need and
desire to be loved
So thank you for making music play over and over in my heart
On this day I wish you wellness and peace in the love I have for you
From self to heart, much peace and love be free
November 25, 2005

Virginia Pulliam

Better With Time

Do you ever pay attention to ageless beauty?
Tree, fine wines a sister in her prime.
Just what age would that be?
Prime time age 25-30
Prime time maturity is 30-40,
40-50 some would like to think you are through (over the hill)
But a sister only gets better with time.
Just watch the sway in her walk, the spark in her eyes,
the strength in her demeanor as she adjusts to any situation.
She has power to save her children from the streets
Work an eight hour jog and please her man in the sheets.
No matter how big or how small,
the problem she will stand by your side.
That's the ageless beauty that gets better with time.
August 1, 2003

Black Sunshine

Your skin is like black sunshine
Sweet and slick like black candy, untouched by time
As I drown myself with thoughts of you,
I bath my body with your smile
In transited by yester years and all the time gone by
The comfort zone of family tides, keeps us close,
knowing not to cross the line
Wow, your skin is like black sunshine,
like the minute before midnight
When good and evil touch, knowing the dawn of your blackness
We continue to play with passionate contentment.
I look into your caramel eyes, the structure cheekbone of your smile, and
the curl of your lashes engulf my being as your thoughts wash over me
We are just to friends whose known each other well and somehow
we know we'll never it there
So I will content myself with dark chocolate, caramel latte twist
I will never cross the line
April 23, 2005

My Friend Sleeps in Kuwait

I sit and wish I was with you and you with me
I sit and wish you could hold my hand, but you are somewhere sleeping in the sand
I sit and wish for shopping spree and cool drinks for you and me
I sit and wish we both could watch the moon not separated by overseas time
I sit and wish for clean sheets and hot water and bubble baths for you
I sit and wish I could see your face and you see mind
I want to do all of the things we used to do
I sit and wish mostly God watches over you, while you sleep and when you are awake
In a land that keeps claming bodies, for what seems like a waste.
I sit and wish for my friend to come back to me, until then you are in my heart and in my prayers
Friendship not changed by overseas time xoxoxooxoxoxoxoxox
April 21, 2005

FIVE

Cute Ass Smile

Did you see that brotha?
With the cute ass smile
The not so tall brotha
Hard body, tight ass, brown skin
Pigeon toes, yeah that's the one
Did you see that brotha?
With the cute ass smile
That's the brotha in my dreams!
Yours too
How about that brotha
With the cute ass smile
The one you take into your dream state
Yes my sista that's the one
Cute ass smile, not so tall, hard body, tight as,
brown skin and pigeon toes.
That's the brotha with the cute ass smile
2003

College Degree

You didn't want to love me for me,
because I didn't have a college degree
Now that the world can see my beauty as thought provoking,
exotic and free
So, now you look at me and tell me you want to get with me
I still don't have a college degree; if you couldn't love me then you
can't get with me now!
Nothing has changed about me except
the world chose to see me for me.
They love me the way I am sensitive,
 passionate, thought provoking and free
All the things I tried to share with you,
 you couldn't love me because I didn't have a college degree
So my brother you still can't get with me
I am so much bigger than your college degree
Don't love me for my resume love me for me
2003

Unhappy Life

I refuse to live an unhappy life
Through your evil ways you ask me to wait
Wait for happiness that will never come
You have no heart or love to give
Your only task is to deceive and have my life stand still
You plague my mind with words that was meant to touch my heart
When only you wish to deceive my only true part
It was all a lie from the start, it was never real love
Just a fairy tale dream no real true parts
My place is not with you, you don't complete the dream, and you
don't make my heart sing
I truly thank you for the time we spent another life lesson for me
Now it's time to walk in the light and let my mind,
body and soul be free
March 15, 2004

My Bread and Butter

There is this place I go that takes me outside of myself
I have to turn myself inside out, I call the place work
I stand outside of myself and watch my daily routine
They keep coming at me, disrespecting,
demeaning and violating my space
Why are you always trying to be in my face?
Why can't they see I am just a sista struggling
trying to make ends meet/
When I see you I don't see a man I see lock-down
That is your uniform of choice and I am quite sure the time, don't
fit the crime.
That's the society we live in, it wasn't create by me
You keep asking me to do things for you, like I can't see that's you
trying to manipulate me
I can't help you this my job, so please why want you just let me be
Who do I look like Harriet Tubman, man see freed the slave
I am just a woman trying to make ends meet
You, want me to show you the real me
Well, that is not for you to see I save that for the free
2000

RAINBOW

Sometimes I sit and wonder
Just where the time has gone
I reach inside and touch myself
I know that another day adorns
What we do today will truly signature tomorrow
I leave my signature on the world
So that all of tomorrow will know a rainbow

Secret

I shared with you my most, darkest secret
The hardest thing for me to do
It took a while to get the words out
I pray to god to help me through
The words came hard like hammers banging in my ears
The pain over whelms me
The look of anticipation in your eyes
Now what do I do
I said the words
If I only knew what you heard
1998

She Loves Her Whatever. What!

She loves her whatever. What!
You can put it in a glass; you can put it in a cup.
When she was a little girl at best, maybe two or was it three?
Why did you come into her room?
Was it to watch her sleep?
Was it to sing her a lullaby or was it to kiss her goodnight?
Daddy's brother is visiting again!
Uncle nightmare is creeping on my skin
Now at thirteen Mr. Art teacher is looking over her shoulder.
She's just a little girl!
Here comes uncle nightmare back to visit again.
Years, gone by she's seventeen.
Her boyfriend left, because she's still a virgin.
No need to ask why!
She's all grown up, all relationship torn.
Sadness creeps through every door.
She's not quite able to fine her place,
but spirit within keeps whispering, Grace!
Secret's being told, silent whispers never heard
The sadness behind those big brown eyes
Oh, how a little girl's pain could never be washed away.
Because no one was ever made to pay!
So now she loves her whatever. What!
You can put it in a glass
But! She prefers hers in a cup.
March 8, 2003

God's Hands

When I was down and all alone
No one to call my very own
I reached-----for the sky
When God gently took my hand
It gave me peace from within and love, sweet honey love
I kindly open my heart, oh so graciously to receive
my part of his blessings
And now, yes now I am feeling, so free

Virginia Pulliam

She Spirit Lives On

The sadness comes with a surprising scream, it turns the room blue
All eyes on me—who new
I am supposed to be the strong one
The words of the doctor haunted my soul, how cruel was his words
Who was he to speak that way about a child I held with love and faith
She's just a child the first born to this young couple
who can not completely understand, why_____
She's barely reached her teens
A diagnosis that would make any heart sad and screech
We processed, what was said
A time for strength and undying Grace
Our minds gathering hope form a higher power as we prayed silently
As the family scattered to gather there thoughts
I find myself standing alone looking into this child's eyes
As she looks back and smiles at me she says "I love you, Auntie"
I smile and hold her hand trying to know how much of this does
she understand
As I reached inside for words nothing greater came than "I love you
too, little girl"
We sit mute for a while as days and nights pass us by
Family and friends came and went and we prayed some more
The treatment came and killed everything that mattered,
even took her hair
Weeks went by – months
Highs and lows of hope and Grace we shared
Until god came in and took over her ride
I sat there by her bedside
Just one more time
As I made my present known
No words came from her lips

She reaches out and touches my hand
As if to say Auntie I am gone
Deaths angel consumed our space, with a gentle brightness
As my child spirit left that room
The Angel of death breezed by my cheek as if to give permission, to
feel a sweet release

**Dedicate to my niece Tacqua Pulliam—September 3, 1983 to
March 14, 1998**

About the Author

The voices inside speaks to me

They voices come from within and speaks to me
They are telling the story from which I come
A little girl, with big brown eyes and caramel skin
Raised on a farm in Chase City, Virginia
Humble beginning with a passion to be heard
Being the middle child, almost never heard
The first born spoiled to death
The last born of seven, loved by all
The middle child searching to find her place
Not feeling the love I raise my voice through my poems
While they continue to speak to me
I will let them be heard
For I am struggling to come out
Never to be lost, silent or in the shadow of others
I will put me passion first and always do my best
For the middle child is who i am, free to me
Virginia Pulliam

I live in Richmond, Virginia
I live my life each day trying to more positive than the day before.
I am a mother, grandmother and friend. I am a woman trying to tap
into her creative nature, by taking classes and bringing positivity in
to my life. I meditate and find quiet time for myself.